HEART OF A
TEACHER

A COLLECTION OF QUOTES AND INSPIRATIONAL STORIES

PAULA J. FOX

simple truths
small books. BIG IMPACT.

Photo Credits
Internals: pages 3, 5-11, 13-21, 23-29, 31-51, 53-61, 63-67, 69-79, 81-85, 87-91, 93-99, 101-109, 111-121, 123-129, 131-137, 140, cajoer/Thinkstock; pages 4, 12, 22, 30, 52, 62, 68, 80, 86, 92, 100, 110, 122, 130, 138, Aerial3/Thinkstock; pages 1-3, 5-11, 13-21, 23-29, 31-51, 53-61, 63-67, 69-79, 81-85, 87-91, 93-99, 101-109, 111-121, 123-129, 131-137, 139-140, Gile68/Thinkstock

Published by Simple Truths, an imprint of Sourcebooks, Inc.
P.O. Box 4410, Naperville, Illinois 60567-4410
(630) 961-3900
Fax: (630) 961-2168
www.sourcebooks.com

Printed and bound China.
LEO 10 9 8 7 6 5 4 3 2 1

FOREWORD

BY MAC ANDERSON,
FOUNDER OF SIMPLE TRUTHS

One of the things I love most about life is that when you wake up each morning, you never know if you might meet someone who will forever make a difference in your life.

It was about to happen on August 19, 2008. On that day, my assistant handed me a stack of mail, and sitting on top of the stack was a letter from Paula Fox, a Simple Truths customer. She said, "Mac, I love your books, and I also love to write poetry. So I wanted to share something I wrote called 'The Second Mile.'"

Well, as you might imagine, we receive a lot of

manuscripts, poems, quotes, and ideas from our customers. Even though I'm grateful for all of them, most do not generate a "wow" response. However, this one did, and I picked up the phone to call Paula.

After a wonderful conversation and discovering that she had been a teacher for thirty years, I asked her if she could write a poem about teaching that we could use in a book we were considering. She said, "Sure, I'd love to!"

The rest, as they say, is history! A few weeks later, she sent me her poem called "Heart of a Teacher." It was absolutely beautiful, and I immediately knew that Paula Fox was the writer I had been looking for to capture the essence of teaching.

On a personal note, however, one of the reasons I wanted to publish a book on teaching was to honor the teachers who had made a difference in my life. I grew up in Trenton, Tennessee, a small town of five thousand people. I have wonderful memories of those first eighteen years. And during those years, there were two teachers who, I can say with certainty, helped make me who I am today.

The first was Ms. Bridges, who taught me in the fourth grade. She was amazing! I'll never forget her beautiful smile and her passion for teaching. She made learning so much fun and made all of us feel as though we could do anything we wanted to do. The positive seeds she planted in my head are still growing!

Then there was Fred Culp, my history teacher in high school. To this day, he is still the funniest person I've ever met. In addition to teaching the history class I loved, he taught me that a sense of humor, especially laughing at yourself, can be one of life's greatest blessings. He also made learning so much more fun than any other teacher I ever had. His class was always the highlight of my day!

So, if you're a teacher, or if, like me, your life was greatly influenced by a teacher, you're going to love this book! The inspirational stories, the photographs, the quotes, and Paula Fox's beautiful, original poems will find a special place in your heart.

Enjoy *Heart of a Teacher*!

THE

faster

YOU GO, THE MORE
STUDENTS YOU LEAVE

BEHIND.

IT DOESN'T MATTER HOW MUCH
OR HOW FAST YOU TEACH.

THE TRUE MEASURE IS HOW
MUCH STUDENTS HAVE

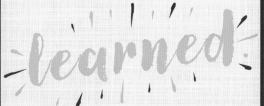

learned

William Glasser

A STUDENT

NEVER

FORGETS AN

Encouraging

PRIVATE WORD,
WHEN IT IS GIVEN WITH

SINCERE

RESPECT &
ADMIRATION.

William Lyon Phelps

FORMAL EDUCATION
WILL MAKE YOU A

LIVING;

SELF-EDUCATION
WILL MAKE YOU A

fortune.

Jim Rohn

It's okay

TO MAKE

MISTAKES.

MISTAKES ARE OUR
TEACHERS—THEY
HELP US

to learn.

John Bradshaw

HEART OF A TEACHER

BY PAULA J. FOX

The child arrives like a mystery box...
    with puzzle pieces inside
some of the pieces are broken or missing...
    and others just seem to hide

But the HEART of a teacher can sort them out...
    and help the child to see
the potential for greatness he has within...
    a picture of what he can be

Her goal isn't just to teach knowledge...
    by filling the box with more parts

it's putting the pieces together...
   to create a work of art

The process is painfully slow at times...
   some need more help than others
each child is a work in progress...
   with assorted shapes and colors

First she creates a classroom...
   where the child can feel safe in school
where he never feels threatened or afraid to try...
   and kindness is always the rule

She knows that a child
   can achieve much more
   when he feels secure inside
when he's valued and loved...
   and believes in himself...
   and he has a sense of pride

She models and teaches good character...
and respect for one another
how to focus on strengths...not weaknesses...
and how to encourage each other

She gives the child the freedom he needs...
to make choices on his own
so he learns to become more responsible...
and is able to stand alone

He's taught to be strong and think for himself
as his soul and spirit heal
and the puzzle that's taking shape inside...
has a much more positive feel

The child discovers the joy that comes
from learning something new...
and his vision grows as he begins
to see all the things he can do

A picture is formed as more pieces fit...
    an image of the child within
with greater strength and confidence...
    and a belief that he can win!

All because a hero was there...
    in the HEART of a teacher who cared
enabling the child to become much more...
    than he ever imagined...or dared

A teacher with a HEART for her children...
    knows what teaching is all about
she may not have all the answers...
    but on this...she has no doubt

When asked which subjects she loved to teach,
    she answered this way and smiled...
"It's not the subjects that matter...
    It's all about teaching the CHILD"

GIVE A MAN A
FISH & YOU FEED
HIM FOR

A DAY.

TEACH A MAN TO
FISH & YOU FEED
HIM FOR A

lifetime.

Proverb

THE WISEST
AND
BEST TEACHERS

TEACH FROM THE

NOT FROM THE

BOOK.

Unknown

IF A CHILD

CAN'T
LEARN

THE WAY WE TEACH, MAYBE
WE SHOULD TEACH THE

way

they

learn.

Ignacio Estrada

CHILDREN HAVE REAL UNDERSTANDING
ONLY OF THAT WHICH THEY

INVENT
THEMSELVES,

AND EACH TIME THAT WE
TRY TO TEACH THEM

TOO QUICKLY,

WE KEEP THEM FROM

reinventing

IT THEMSELVES.

Jean Piaget

ONE LOOKS BACK WITH

APPRECIATION

TO THE BRILLIANT TEACHERS, BUT WITH
GRATITUDE TO THOSE WHO TOUCHED OUR

human feelings

THE CURRICULUM IS SO MUCH
NECESSARY RAW MATERIAL, BUT

WARMTH

IS THE VITAL ELEMENT FOR THE GROWING
PLANT AND FOR THE SOUL OF THE CHILD.

Carl Jung

BEAUTIFUL CRAYONS

 BY PAULA J. FOX

I believe that every child is special and has something of value to contribute to our world. I wrote this poem as a reminder that it is our job as teachers to help everyone in our class to feel needed and important...because they are!!

Every year brings a new class of students...
    like crayons we find in school
    assorted sizes, shapes, and colors
    some are warm...some totally cool

Some are sharp...some very dull...
     some lost along the way
     Some have a bright and cheerful tone
     others more dark and grey

They all have names...some are common ones...
     easy to recognize
     Others are weird and hard to pronounce
     all special in God's eyes

Some of them...look fresh and new...
     while others appear well worn
     Some are shiny...some have sparkles
     many are broken and torn

But each one plays an important part...
     regardless of appearance
     as together they create a masterpiece
     with contrast, shadows, and brilliance

If we only used our favorite colors...
    and excluded all the rest
    our artwork would be boring
    and we'd miss out on God's best

It takes ALL the colors in the rainbow...
    with each varied tone and hue
    to give depth and meaning to our picture
    and enrich our point of view

It's the same with the children God created...
    each has something to give
    adding value and beauty in their own way
    to the world in which we live

Education

IS THE KEY TO

UNLOCK

THE GOLDEN DOOR OF

freedom.

George Washington Carver

JUST REMEMBER THE
WORLD IS NOT A

PLAYGROUND

BUT A

SCHOOLROOM.

LIFE IS NOT A

HOLIDAY

BUT AN

EDUCATION.

ONE ETERNAL LESSON FOR US ALL: TO
TEACH US HOW BETTER WE SHOULD

love.

Barbara Jordan

TEACHING IS LEAVING A

vestige

OF ONESELF IN THE DEVELOPMENT
OF ANOTHER. AND
SURELY THE STUDENT IS

A BANK

WHERE YOU CAN DEPOSIT
YOUR MOST PRECIOUS

treasures.

Eugene P. Bertin

THE ABILITY TO

learn

IS OLDER—AS IT IS
ALSO

MORE

WIDESPREAD—THAN
IS THE ABILITY TO

teach

Margaret Mead

MARK EKLUND: A TRUE STORY ABOUT A ONE-IN-A-MILLION STUDENT

 BY SISTER HELEN MROSLA

He was in the first third grade class I taught at Saint Mary's School in Morris, Minnesota. All thirty-four of my students were dear to me, but Mark Eklund was one in a million. Very neat in appearance, he had that happy-to-be-alive attitude that made even his occasional mischievousness delightful.

Mark talked incessantly. I had to remind him again and again that talking without permission was not acceptable. What impressed me so much, though, was his sincere response every time I had to correct him for misbehaving. "Thank you for correcting me, Sister!" I didn't know what to make of it at first, but before long, I became accustomed to hearing it many times a day.

One morning, my patience was growing thin when Mark talked once too often, and then I made a novice teacher's mistake. I looked at Mark and said, "If you say one more word, I am going to tape your mouth shut!" It wasn't ten seconds later when Chuck blurted out, "Mark is talking again." I hadn't asked any of the students to help me watch Mark, but since I had stated the punishment in front of the class, I had to act on it. I remember the scene as if it had occurred this morning. I walked to my desk, very deliberately opened my drawer, and took out a roll of masking tape. Without saying a word, I proceeded to Mark's desk, tore off two pieces of tape, and made a big X with them over his mouth. I then returned to the front of the room. As I glanced at Mark to see how he was doing, he winked at me. That did it! I started laughing. The class cheered as I walked back to Mark's desk, removed the tape, and shrugged my shoulders. His first words were, "Thank you for correcting me, Sister."

At the end of the year, I was asked to teach junior-high math. The years flew by, and before I knew it, Mark was in my classroom again. He was more handsome than ever and just as polite. Since he had to listen carefully to my instruction in the "new math," he did not talk as much in ninth grade as he had in third. One Friday, things just didn't feel right. We had worked hard on a new concept all week, and I sensed that the students were frowning, frustrated with themselves and edgy with one another. I had to stop this crankiness before it got out of hand. So I asked them to list the names of the other students in the room on two sheets of paper, leaving a space between each name. Then I told them to think of the nicest thing they could say about each of their classmates and write it down. It took the remainder of the class period to finish the assignment, and as the students left the room, each one handed me the papers. Charlie smiled. Mark said, "Thank you for teaching me, Sister. Have a good weekend." That Saturday, I wrote down the name of each student on a separate sheet of paper, and I listed what everyone else had said about that individual.

On Monday, I gave each student his or her list. Before long, the entire class was smiling. "Really?" I heard whispered. "I never knew that meant anything to anyone!" "I didn't know others liked me so much." No one ever mentioned those papers in class again. I never knew if they discussed them after class or with their parents, but it didn't matter. The exercise had accomplished its purpose. The students were happy with themselves and one another again.

That group of students moved on. Several years later, after I returned from vacation, my parents met me at the airport. As we were driving home, Mother asked me the usual questions about the trip, the weather, my experiences in general. There was a lull in the conversation. Mother gave Dad a sideways glance and simply said, "Dad?" My father cleared his throat, as he usually did before saying something important.

"The Eklunds called last night," he began.

"Really?" I said. "I haven't heard from them in years. I wonder how Mark is."

Dad responded quietly. "Mark was killed in Vietnam," he said. "The funeral is tomorrow, and his parents would like it if you could attend."

To this day, I can still point to the exact spot on I-494 where Dad told me about Mark.

I had never seen a serviceman in a military coffin before. Mark looked so handsome, so mature. All I could think at that moment was, *Mark, I would give all the masking tape in the world if only you would talk to me.* The church was packed with Mark's friends. Chuck's sister sang "The Battle Hymn of the Republic." Why did it have to rain on the day of the funeral? It was difficult enough at the graveside. The pastor said the usual prayers, and the bugler played "Taps." One by one, those who loved Mark took a last walk by the coffin and sprinkled it with holy water. I was the last one to bless the coffin. As I stood there, one of the soldiers who acted as pallbearer came up to me. "Were you Mark's math teacher?" he asked. I nodded as I continued to stare at the coffin. "Mark talked about you a lot," he said.

After the funeral, most of Mark's former classmates headed to Chuck's farmhouse for lunch. Mark's mother and father were there, obviously waiting for me. "We want to show you something," his father said, taking a wallet out of his pocket. "They found this on Mark when he was killed. We thought you might recognize it." Opening the billfold, he carefully removed two worn pieces of notebook paper that had obviously been taped, folded, and refolded many times. I knew without looking that the papers were the ones on which I had listed all the good things each of Mark's classmates had said about him.

"Thank you so much for doing that," Mark's mother said. "As you can see, Mark treasured it."

Mark's classmates started to gather around us. Charlie smiled rather sheepishly and said, "I still have my list. I keep it in the top drawer of my desk at home."

Chuck's wife said, "Chuck asked me to put his in our wedding album."

"I have mine too—in my diary," Marilyn said. Then Vicki, another classmate, reached into her pocketbook, took out her wallet, and showed her worn and frazzled list to the group. "I carry this with me at all times," Vicki said without batting an eyelash.

"I think we all saved our lists." That's when I finally sat down and cried. I cried for Mark and for all his friends who would never see him again.

The density of people in society is so thick that we forget that life will end one day. And we don't know when that one day will be. So please, tell the people you love and care for that they are special and important. Tell them, before it is too late.

MOST OF US END UP WITH

NO MORE

THAN FIVE OR SIX PEOPLE
THAT REMEMBER US.
TEACHERS HAVE

thousands

OF PEOPLE WHO

REMEMBER

THEM FOR THE REST
OF THEIR LIVES.

Andrew A. Rooney

THEY MAY FORGET

WHAT
YOU SAID...

BUT THEY WILL

NEVER

FORGET HOW YOU MADE THEM

feel.

Carl W. Buehner

EACH SECOND WE LIVE IS A NEW AND

unique
moment

OF THE UNIVERSE, A MOMENT THAT
WILL NEVER BE AGAIN. AND WHAT DO WE TEACH
OUR CHILDREN IN SCHOOL? WE TEACH THEM
THAT TWO AND TWO MAKE FOUR, AND THAT
PARIS IS THE CAPITAL OF FRANCE. WHEN WILL
WE ALSO TEACH THEM WHAT THEY ARE? WE
SHOULD SAY TO EACH OF THEM: DO YOU
KNOW WHAT YOU ARE?
YOU ARE A

MARVEL.

YOU ARE

UNIQUE.

IN ALL THE YEARS THAT HAVE
PASSED, THERE HAS

NEVER

BEEN ANOTHER CHILD LIKE YOU.
YOUR LEGS, YOUR ARMS, YOUR
CUNNING FINGERS, THE WAY YOU
MOVE! YOU MAY BE A SHAKESPEARE,
A MICHELANGELO, A BEETHOVEN. YOU
HAVE THE CAPACITY FOR ANYTHING. YES,

YOU ARE A
MARVEL.

AND WHEN YOU GROW UP, CAN YOU THEN
HARM ANOTHER WHO IS, LIKE YOU, A MARVEL?
YOU MUST WORK, WE MUST ALL WORK,
TO MAKE THE WORLD

worthy of its children.

Pablo Casals

I touch

THE FUTURE.

I teach.

Christa McAuliffe

TEACHING IS THE

GREATEST

ACT OF

optimism.

Colleen Wilcox

IF WE DO NOT

INTENTIONALLY

add value

TO OTHERS, WE PROBABLY

UNINTENTIONALLY

subtract

FROM THEM.

John C. Maxwell

A

NEGATIVE

OUTLOOK IS MORE OF A

handicap

THAN ANY

PHYSICAL
INJURY.

Christopher Paolini

WHO

dares

TO TEACH MUST

NEVER

CEASE TO

learn.

John C. Dana

THE MEDIOCRE TEACHER

TELLS.

THE GOOD TEACHER

EXPLAINS.

THE SUPERIOR TEACHER

DEMONSTRATES.

THE GREAT TEACHER

inspires.

William Arthur Ward

THE

good life

IS ONE
INSPIRED BY

LOVE

AND GUIDED BY

KNOWLEDGE.

Bertrand Russell

IT WAS A

HIGH
COUNSEL

THAT I ONCE HEARD GIVEN TO A
YOUNG PERSON,

"ALWAYS DO
WHAT YOU ARE

TO DO."

Ralph Waldo Emerson

HE THAT TEACHES US
ANYTHING WHICH
WE KNEW

not

BEFORE IS
UNDOUBTEDLY
TO BE REVERENCED
AS A

MASTER.

Samuel Johnson

EVERY TRUTH HAS

FOUR CORNERS:

AS A TEACHER I GIVE YOU

ONE CORNER,

AND IT IS FOR YOU
TO FIND THE

other
three.

Confucius

THE CREATION OF A TEACHER

 UNKNOWN

The Good Lord was creating teachers. It was His sixth day of "overtime," and He knew that this was a tremendous responsibility, for teachers would touch the lives of so many impressionable young children. An angel appeared to Him and said, "You are taking a long time to figure this one out."

"Yes," said the Lord, "but have you read the specs on this order?"

A TEACHER:

- Must stand above all students, yet be on their level
- Must be able to do 180 things not connected with the subject being taught
- Must run on caffeine and leftovers
- Must communicate vital knowledge to all students daily and be right most of the time
- Must have more time for others than for herself/himself
- Must have a smile that can endure through pay cuts, problematic children, and worried parents
- Must go on teaching when parents and mandates question every move
- Must have six pairs of hands

"Six pairs of hands," said the angel. "That's impossible."

"Well," said the Lord, "it is not the hands that are the problem. It is the three pairs of eyes that are presenting the most difficulty!"

The angel looked incredulous, "Three pairs of eyes... on a standard model?"

The Lord nodded His head. "One pair can see a student for what he is and not what others have labeled him as. Another pair of eyes is in the back of the teacher's head to see what should not be seen but what must be known. The eyes in the front are only to look at the child as he/she 'acts out' in order to reflect, 'I understand and I still believe in you,' without so much as saying a word to the child."

"Lord," said the angel, "this is a very large project, and I think you should work on it tomorrow."

"I can't," said the Lord, "for I have come very close to creating something much like Myself. I have one that comes to work when he/she is sick, teaches a class of children that do not want to learn, has a special place in his/her heart for children who are not his/her own, understands the struggles of those who have difficulty, and never takes the students for granted."

The angel looked closely at the model the Lord was creating and said, "It is too softhearted."

"Yes," said the Lord, "but also tough. You cannot imagine what this teacher can endure or do, if necessary."

"Can this teacher think?" asked the angel.

"Not only think," said the Lord, "but reason and compromise."

The angel came closer to have a better look at the model and ran his finger over the teacher's cheek.

"Well, Lord," said the angel, "your job looks fine, but there is a leak. I told you that you were putting too much into this model. You cannot imagine the stress that will be placed upon the teacher."

The Lord moved in closer and lifted the drop of moisture from the teacher's cheek. It shone and glistened in the light. "It is not a leak," He said. "It is a tear."

"A tear? What is that?" asked the angel. "What is a tear for?"

The Lord replied with great thought, "It is for the joy and pride of seeing a child accomplish even the smallest task. It is for the loneliness of children who have a hard time fitting in, and it is for compassion for the feelings of their parents. It comes from the pain of not being able to reach some children and the disappointment those children feel in themselves. It comes often when a teacher has been with a class for a year and must say good-bye to those students and get ready to welcome a new class."

"My," said the angel, "the tear thing is a great idea. You are a genius!"

The Lord looked somber. "I didn't put it there."

THOSE WHO CAN,

do...

THOSE WHO CAN
DO MORE,

TEACH.

Unknown

EVERY CHILD'S LIFE
IS LIKE A

PIECE OF
PAPER

ON WHICH EVERY
PERSON LEAVES A

mark.

Chinese proverb

TO ME, EDUCATION IS A

leading out

OF WHAT IS

ALREADY
THERE

IN THE PUPIL'S SOUL.

Muriel Spark

WHAT OFFICE IS THERE
WHICH INVOLVES MORE

responsibility,

WHICH REQUIRES MORE

QUALIFICATIONS,

AND WHICH OUGHT, THEREFORE,
TO BE MORE

honorable,

THAN THAT OF TEACHING?

Harriet Martineau

HANDLE WITH CARE

 BY PAULA J. FOX

A child's heart is fragile...
  don't break it
A child's mind is open...
  don't close it
A child's soul is tender...
  don't harden it
A child's spirit is joyful...
  don't crush it

I LIKE

nonsense,

IT WAKES UP THE
BRAIN CELLS. FANTASY IS A

NECESSARY

INGREDIENT IN LIVING.
IT'S A WAY OF LOOKING AT LIFE
THROUGH THE WRONG END OF A
TELESCOPE, WHICH IS WHAT I DO,
AND THAT ENABLES YOU TO

laugh

AT LIFE'S REALITIES.

Theodor "Dr. Seuss" Geisel

EDUCATION CAN BE DEFINED AS

WORKING

WITH PEOPLE, YOUNG AND OLD,
TO PREPARE THEM

IN THE FUTURE. THE FUTURE MAY
BE BRIGHT. THE FUTURE MAY BE
GRAY. BUT, MOST IMPORTANTLY
WE MUST INSURE THAT THERE

WILL BE

A FUTURE.

Willard J. Jacobson

A GOOD TEACHER IS ONE WHO

YOU BECOME WHO YOU

FEEL YOURSELF TO BE.

A GOOD TEACHER IS ALSO ONE
WHO SAYS SOMETHING THAT YOU

WON'T UNDERSTAND

UNTIL TEN YEARS LATER.

Julius Lester

IN SEEKING WISDOM,
THE FIRST STEP IS

SILENCE,

THE SECOND

LISTENING,

THE THIRD

REMEMBERING,

THE FOURTH

PRACTICING,

THE FIFTH—

teaching
others.

Solomon ibn Gabriol

UPSIDE DOWN DAYS

 BY PAULA J. FOX

We call them "upside down days"...when things
    just fall apart
    and nothing seems to go the way it's planned
Normal schedules get mixed up and kids seem to forget
    the classroom rules they used to understand

That's when creative teachers will turn things
    "upside down"
    making it a game for just one day

Completely changing everything...and the order
    things are done
      doing routine tasks a different way

Just thinking of things "upside down" makes
    everything more fun
      kids smile when they are more inclined to frown
Mistakes don't seem like problems then...
    they take things more in stride
They can laugh and work at turning things around

Sometimes the lessons taught in school aren't
    always found in books...
      important things like...F L E X I B I L I T Y
And nothing helps to make the point like showing
    how it's done...
      making "upside down days"...FUN! ...like they
    should be!

A GIFTED TEACHER MAKES
LEARNING A JOY BY

CAPTURING

TEACHABLE MOMENTS AND
TURNING THEM INTO

magical

LEARNING EXPERIENCES.

THE WISE IN HEART
ARE CALLED

Discerning,

AND GRACIOUS WORDS
PROMOTE

instruction.

Proverbs 16:21

YOU CAN TEACH A
STUDENT A LESSON

for a day;

BUT IF YOU CAN TEACH
HIM TO LEARN BY

**CREATING
CURIOSITY,**

HE WILL CONTINUE THE
LEARNING PROCESS

*as long as
he lives.*

Clay P. Bedford

WHAT THE TEACHER IS

IS

MORE
IMPORTANT

THAN

*what he
teaches.*

Karl A. Menninger

TELL ME AND

I FORGET.

TEACH ME AND

I REMEMBER.

INVOLVE ME AND

I learn.

Xun Kuang

WHAT WE

become

DEPENDS ON WHAT WE

READ

AFTER ALL THE PROFESSORS
HAVE FINISHED WITH US. THE
GREATEST UNIVERSITY OF ALL IS A

COLLECTION
OF BOOKS.

Thomas Carlyle

THE GREATEST

SIGN

OF SUCCESS FOR A TEACHER
IS TO BE ABLE TO SAY,
"THE CHILDREN ARE NOW
WORKING AS IF I

*did not
exist."*

Maria Montessori

OUR GREATEST

NATURAL
RESOURCE

IS THE

minds

OF OUR CHILDREN.

Walt Disney

CREATIVE TEACHERS DON'T
JUST FOCUS ON THE

DESTINATION...

THEY MAKE THE

JOURNEY

"WHOSE CHILD IS THIS?"

UNKNOWN

"Whose child is this?" I asked one day
Seeing a little one out at play
"Mine," said the parent with a tender smile
"Mine to keep a little while
To bathe his hands and comb his hair
To tell him what he is to wear
To prepare him that he may always be good
And each day do the things he should"

"Whose child is this?" I asked again
As the door opened and someone came in

"Mine," said the teacher with the same tender smile
"Mine, to keep just for a little while
To teach him how to be gentle and kind
To train and direct his dear little mind
To help him live by every rule
And get the best he can from school"

"Whose child is this?" I asked once more
Just as the little one entered the door
"Ours," said the parent and the teacher as they smiled
And each took the hand of the little child
"Ours to love and train together
Ours this blessed task forever."

NO ONE HAS YET FULLY REALIZED THE

WEALTH OF
SYMPATHY,

THE KINDNESS AND GENEROSITY
HIDDEN IN THE SOUL OF A CHILD.
THE EFFORT OF EVERY TRUE
EDUCATOR SHOULD BE TO

UNLOCK

THAT

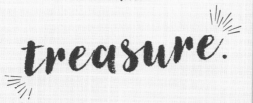

treasure.

Sebastian Faure

CREATIVE ACTIVITY COULD BE
DESCRIBED AS A TYPE OF

LEARNING
PROCESS

WHERE TEACHER AND PUPIL
ARE LOCATED IN THE

same

individual

Arthur Koestler

ONE OF THE BEAUTIES OF
TEACHING IS THAT THERE IS

NO LIMIT

TO ONE'S GROWTH AS A
TEACHER, JUST AS THERE IS NO
KNOWING BEFOREHAND

HOW MUCH

YOUR STUDENTS

can learn.

Herbert Kohl

A PARENT'S NOTE TO A TEACHER

ANONYMOUS

I'm the voice of a grateful parent
whose child was in your class...
the one who needed help to find his way

You've been a special blessing
as you helped my child succeed
and I'm thankful for the part you had to play

You gave him so much more
than just the lessons in the books
you gave him wings...so he could learn to fly

You ignited a flame within his soul

a passion to learn and grow…

to never give up and always be willing to try

Your encouragement inspired him

and your kindness was so real

but the thing that thrills my heart the most

is this…

By building his self-confidence

you changed his life this year

he believes in himself…and a brighter future

is his!

I'VE COME TO THE FRIGHTENING CONCLUSION THAT I AM THE

DECISIVE ELEMENT

IN THE CLASSROOM. IT'S MY DAILY MOOD THAT MAKES THE WEATHER. AS A TEACHER, I POSSESS A TREMENDOUS POWER TO MAKE A CHILD'S LIFE MISERABLE OR JOYOUS. I CAN BE A TOOL OF TORTURE OR AN INSTRUMENT OF INSPIRATION. I CAN HUMILIATE OR HUMOR, HURT OR HEAL. IN ALL SITUATIONS, IT IS

my response

THAT DECIDES WHETHER A CRISIS WILL BE ESCALATED OR DE-ESCALATED AND A CHILD HUMANIZED OR DE-HUMANIZED.

Haim Ginott

THE AIM OF EDUCATION SHOULD
BE TO TEACH US RATHER

HOW TO THINK,

THAN WHAT TO THINK, RATHER TO
IMPROVE OUR MINDS, SO AS
TO ENABLE US TO

think for ourselves,

THAN TO LOAD THE MEMORY WITH
THE THOUGHTS OF OTHER MEN.

James Beattie

CULTIVATE YOUR GARDEN.

**DO NOT DEPEND
UPON TEACHERS**

TO EDUCATE YOU_
FOLLOW YOUR OWN BENT,

pursue

YOUR CURIOSITY BRAVELY,
EXPRESS YOURSELF,
MAKE YOUR OWN HARMONY.

Will Durant

RAINBOW MOMENT

 BY PAULA J. FOX

There is something about a rainbow that is so
breathtaking it causes most people to stop what
they are doing and look,
even if just for a moment.
And that moment we stop and look refreshes our soul.

Children love to stop and look at many things
that adults would just ignore and pass right on by.
But a rainbow moment…and the beauty and benefit
of living in that moment…
is fleeting and will soon be gone.

Children often learn best in those spontaneous moments
when they want to stop and look.
Their natural curiosity makes them want to stop
whatever they're doing and find out more
about something that interests them.
We call these "teachable moments" for obvious reasons.

The lesson in the rainbow is that
it's important to stop and look...
and teach the child what he's interested in experiencing
and learning at that moment,
because the teachable moment can't
be recaptured later.

WITHOUT BOOKS

THE DEVELOPMENT OF
CIVILIZATION WOULD HAVE BEEN

impossible.

THEY ARE ENGINES OF CHANGE,
WINDOWS OF THE WORLD, AND (AS A
POET HAS SAID) "LIGHTHOUSES ERECTED
IN THE SEA OF TIME." THEY ARE
COMPANIONS, TEACHERS, MAGICIANS,
BANKERS OF THE TREASURES OF
THE MIND. BOOKS ARE

HUMANITY
IN PRINT.

Barbara Tuchman

DON'T

limit

A CHILD TO

YOUR OWN
LEARNING,

FOR HE WAS BORN IN

*another
time.*

Unknown

EDUCATION IS THE

LEADING OF
HUMAN SOULS

TO WHAT IS

best,

AND MAKING WHAT IS BEST

OUT OF
THEM.

John Ruskin

YOU CAN'T TEACH PEOPLE

EVERYTHING THEY NEED TO KNOW.

THE BEST YOU CAN DO IS POSITION THEM WHERE THEY CAN

WHAT THEY NEED TO KNOW WHEN THEY NEED TO KNOW IT.

Seymour Papert

THE WORK

WILL WAIT

WHILE YOU SHOW THE CHILD
THE RAINBOW, BUT
THE RAINBOW WON'T
WAIT WHILE YOU

do the
work.

Patricia Clafford

THE ANIMAL SCHOOL

BY GEORGE H. REAVIS

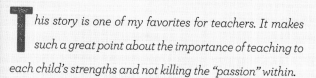

T his story is one of my favorites for teachers. It makes such a great point about the importance of teaching to each child's strengths and not killing the "passion" within.

Once upon a time, the animals decided they must do something heroic to meet the problems of "a new world." So they organized a school.

They adopted an activity curriculum consisting of running, climbing, swimming, and flying. To make it easier to administer the curriculum, all the animals took all the subjects.

The duck was excellent in swimming, in fact better than his instructor, but he made only passing grades in flying and was very poor in running. Since he was slow in running, he had to stay after school and also drop swimming in order to practice running. This was kept up until his webbed feet were badly worn and he was only average in swimming. But average was acceptable in school, so nobody worried about that except the duck.

The rabbit started at the top of the class in running but had a nervous breakdown because of so much makeup work in swimming.

The squirrel was excellent in climbing until he developed frustration in the flying class, where his teacher made him start from the ground up instead of from the treetop down. He also developed a charley horse from overexertion and then got a C in climbing and a D in running.

The eagle was a problem child and was disciplined severely. In the climbing class, he beat all the others to the top of the tree but insisted on using his own way to get there.

At the end of the year, an abnormal eel that could swim exceedingly well and also run, climb, and fly a little had the highest average and was valedictorian.

The prairie dogs stayed out of school and fought the tax levy because the administration would not add digging and burrowing to the curriculum. They apprenticed their children to a badger and later joined the groundhogs and gophers to start a successful private school.

ALTHOUGH IT IS THE

SMALLEST

OF ALL SEEDS, IT GROWS

LARGER

THAN ANY GARDEN PLANT
AND BECOMES A

tree.

Matthew 13:32

I'M

NOT

A TEACHER, BUT AN

awakener.

Robert Frost

NINE

TENTHS

OF EDUCATION IS

encouragement.

Anatole France

IT IS THE MARK OF AN
EDUCATED MIND TO BE ABLE TO

ENTERTAIN
A THOUGHT

WITHOUT

accepting it.

Aristotle

CHILDREN ARE APT

to live
up to

WHAT YOU

BELIEVE
OF
THEM.

Lady Bird Johnson

THE MOST EXTRAORDINARY
THING ABOUT

A REALLY GOOD TEACHER

IS THAT HE OR SHE

transcends

ACCEPTED EDUCATIONAL
METHODS. SUCH METHODS ARE
DESIGNED TO HELP AVERAGE
TEACHERS APPROXIMATE THE
PERFORMANCE OF
GOOD TEACHERS.

Margaret Mead

A LOVING TEACHER

 BY PAT MCCLAIN

Things our grown-up mind defies
Appear as giants in children's eyes.
A gentle touch upon her head
A simple word when kindly said.

Complete attention when she calls
Her knowing you have given all.
Correcting in a loving way.
Instilling trust in what you say.

Making her believe unique
The tiny flaw upon her cheek.

Admiring old and faded dresses.
Reminding her we all make messes.

Words of comfort you've softly spoken
A promise you've made
She knows won't be broken.
Your knowing her doll that was lost today
Is just as important as bills you can't pay.

Helping make her plans and schemes
Giving her hope and building her dreams.
All of this and so much more
Is in her mind forever stored.

They who touch her life awhile
Can either make or break that child.
Education is important, true,
But so much more, her faith in you.

You've weathered through the storm and strife;
You helped to build a small girl's life.
You're truly one to be admired.
For you gave more than was required.

ONE SPECIAL TEACHER
CAN MAKE A

POSITIVE
DIFFERENCE

IN A CHILD'S
ENTIRE LIFE IN JUST

one year!

WE NOW ACCEPT THE FACT THAT
LEARNING IS A

LIFELONG
PROCESS

OF KEEPING ABREAST OF

AND THE MOST PRESSING TASK
IS TO TEACH PEOPLE

HOW TO
LEARN.

Peter F. Drucker

A TEACHER
IS ONE
WHO MAKES HIMSELF

PROGRESSIVELY

unnecessary.

Thomas Carruthers

PERHAPS THE MOST VALUABLE RESULT
OF ALL EDUCATION IS THE ABILITY
TO MAKE YOURSELF

DO THE THING
YOU HAVE TO DO,

WHEN IT OUGHT TO BE DONE,
WHETHER YOU LIKE IT OR NOT.
IT IS THE FIRST LESSON THAT OUGHT
TO BE LEARNED; AND HOWEVER EARLY A
MAN'S TRAINING BEGINS, IT IS PROBABLY

the last
lesson

THAT HE LEARNS THOROUGHLY.

Thomas H. Huxley

IF YOUR PLAN IS FOR ONE YEAR,

PLANT RICE;

IF YOUR PLAN IS FOR TEN YEARS,

PLANT TREES;

IF YOUR PLAN IS FOR
ONE HUNDRED YEARS,

*educate
children.*

Confucius

WHEN THE
STUDENT IS

ready,

THE TEACHER WILL

APPEAR.

Unknown

AN EDUCATION ISN'T HOW MUCH
YOU HAVE COMMITTED TO
MEMORY, OR EVEN HOW MUCH
YOU KNOW. IT'S BEING ABLE TO

differentiate

BETWEEN

WHAT YOU
DO KNOW

AND

WHAT YOU
DON'T.

William Feather

EDUCATION IS WHAT

AFTER ONE HAS

FORGOTTEN

WHAT ONE HAS
LEARNED IN SCHOOL.

Unknown

A TEACHER'S DASH

BY LINDA ELLIS

It's been said the dash on a headstone
between the dates of birth and death
represents each step we'll take on earth...
and every single breath.

We know the date when we were born,
but the following date can't be foreseen
and all the days that we will live
are in that little dash in between.

Though we all may strive to prosper
during our time here on earth,

it isn't the money in our bank account
that measures what our dash is worth.

Some deem themselves "successful"
if they can spend in large amounts,
but how you spend your only dash
is all that really counts.

When young minds want to understand
what is just beyond their reach,
a special soul is called upon
to enlighten…and to teach.

A teacher chooses her career
not for prestige, wealth, or cash,
but because her heart is telling her
this is how to live her dash.

For she receives true satisfaction
from guiding and from giving;
fulfillment found in making a life...
and not just making a living.

A good teacher has a tendency
to do more than what's required
to prepare and send into the world
each "dash" that she's inspired.

Teachers make a difference
in each young mind they embrace;
they mold our future in their classrooms
and make the world a better place.

THERE ARE TWO EDUCATIONS.
ONE SHOULD TEACH US

HOW TO MAKE A LIVING

AND THE OTHER

how to live.

James Truslow Adams

WHAT WE WANT IS TO SEE THE

CHILD IN PURSUIT OF KNOWLEDGE,

AND NOT

KNOWLEDGE

in pursuit

OF THE CHILD.

George Bernard Shaw

TEACHERS WHO
EDUCATE CHILDREN

deserve

MORE HONOR THAN PARENTS
WHO MERELY GAVE BIRTH. FOR
BARE LIFE IS FURNISHED BY
THE ONE, THE OTHER ENSURES A

GOOD

LIFE.

Aristotle

TEACHERS MAY

NOT

MAKE A LOT OF

money...

BUT THEY MAKE

A LOT

OF

difference.

THE GIFT OF A TEACHER'S HEART

 BY PAULA J. FOX

When God was designing talents and gifts...
  He carefully crafted each one
but the Heart that He made for the Gift of Teaching...
  was beyond comparison!

He saved this important gift for last...
  spending time on every feature
creating His very best design
  for the special **Heart of a Teacher**

It's a **Heart of Humility** focused on others...
  unselfish in all its ways

with a spirit of love and gratitude
    never seeking to receive the praise

It's a **Heart of Generosity**…
    that gives more than the job will pay
It's not about money…
    but touching lives that may change the world
    someday

It's a **Heart of Joy** that makes learning fun…
    and finds delight in teaching
creating and capturing teachable moments
    for exploring…learning…reaching

It's a **Heart of Wisdom** that teaches truth…
    and accountability too
building character and integrity
    so each child will know what to do

It's a **Heart of Kindness** that's sensitive...
  to the feelings of a child
adding value and building self-confidence
  with encouraging words and a smile

It's a **Heart of Compassion** that reaches out...
  to the child with special needs
helping to overcome challenges
  making sure that he succeeds

It's a **Heart of Discernment** that understands...
  and has the insight to see
beyond what a child is like today
  to his potential...and what he can be

It's a **Heart of Purpose** that knows what matters...
  is the treasure inside every heart
helping each child to find his own way
  to play a significant part

It's a **Heart of Passion** that inspires greatness...
   by lighting a fire within
empowering a child with the inner strength
   to go further than he's ever been

It's a **Heart of Patience** that never gives up...
   when the process seems much too slow
always searching for better solutions
   to help a child learn and grow

It's not easy being a Teacher...
   and this Heart takes a beating each day
sometimes it breaks for a hurting child
   and a piece is given away

But there's strength in the **Heart of a Teacher...**
   and a special vision to see
the difference you make in the heart of a child...
   can affect eternity!

A HUNDRED YEARS
FROM NOW, IT WILL

NOT MATTER

WHAT MY BANK ACCOUNT WAS,
THE SORT OF HOUSE I LIVED IN,
OR THE KIND OF CAR I DROVE.
BUT THE WORLD MAY BE
DIFFERENT BECAUSE I WAS

important

IN THE LIFE OF

A CHILD.

Forest E. Witcraft

WHAT

SCULPTURE

IS TO A BLOCK OF MARBLE,

EDUCATION

IS TO A

human

soul.

Joseph Addison

EVERY CHILD MUST BE

ENCOURAGED

TO GET AS MUCH EDUCATION AS HE HAS
THE ABILITY TO TAKE. WE WANT THIS NOT
ONLY FOR HIS SAKE—BUT FOR THE

nation's sake.

NOTHING MATTERS MORE TO THE FUTURE OF
OUR COUNTRY; NOT MILITARY PREPAREDNESS—FOR
ARMED MIGHT IS WORTHLESS IF WE LACK THE BRAIN
POWER TO BUILD A WORLD OF PEACE; NOT OUR
PRODUCTIVE ECONOMY—FOR WE CANNOT SUSTAIN
GROWTH WITHOUT TRAINED MANPOWER; NOT OUR
DEMOCRATIC SYSTEM OF GOVERNMENT—FOR

FREEDOM
IS FRAGILE

IF CITIZENS ARE IGNORANT.

Lyndon B. Johnson

ABOUT THE AUTHOR

Paula J. Fox describes herself as a lifetime student whose passion is to continue learning and applying godly wisdom in her life so that she can share it with others. Her desire is to inspire and motivate others to live a life of purpose and significance. She is a teacher at heart with a degree in special education and thirty-five years of experience teaching and leading all ages from preschool through adult.

She and her husband, Larry, have three grown

children, and she is now able to devote more of her time to writing. Besides being a teacher and leader in her own church, she is the founder and leader of L'dor (Ladies' day of renewal), a home-based Bible study for women. This ministry, which began more than twenty-five years ago, meets weekly in homes where they worship together through songs and scriptures, sharing and studying God's Word together. Paula loves researching and writing her own lessons for L'dor as well as writing poetry and prose. She also enjoys speaking to women's groups and retreats.

Contact Paula Fox at paulajfox@live.com.

LET NO ONE EVER COME TO YOU
WITHOUT LEAVING

BETTER
AND
HAPPIER.

BE THE LIVING EXPRESSION OF GOD'S
KINDNESS: KINDNESS IN YOUR FACE,
KINDNESS IN YOUR EYES, KINDNESS
IN YOUR SMILE, KINDNESS IN YOUR

warm greeting.

Mother Teresa

EDUCATION IS AN IMPORTANT
ELEMENT IN THE STRUGGLE FOR

human
rights.

IT IS THE MEANS TO HELP OUR CHILDREN
AND PEOPLE REDISCOVER THEIR
IDENTITY AND THEREBY INCREASE
SELF-RESPECT. EDUCATION IS OUR

PASSPORT

TO THE FUTURE, FOR TOMORROW
BELONGS TO THE PEOPLE WHO
PREPARE FOR IT TODAY.

Malcolm X

NEVER LET A SINGLE DAY PASS
WITHOUT SAYING AN

encouraging
 word

TO EACH CHILD. "MORE PEOPLE
FAIL FOR LACK OF
ENCOURAGEMENT," SOMEONE
WROTE, "THAN FOR

ANY

OTHER REASON."

Ruth Bell Graham

CHANGE STARTS WITH
SOMETHING SIMPLE.

▷Shop for books on themes like: teamwork, success, leadership, customer service, motivation, and more.

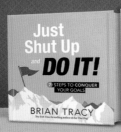

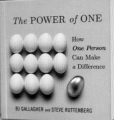

Pick from hundreds of titles at:
SimpleTruths.com

Call us toll-free at **1-800-900-3427**